THE UNREAL WORLD OF SOCIAL MEDIA

By

H.H. HACHEM

INTRODUCTION

The wonderful world of Social Media has the entire universe by the balls. In the era of post-2000 life, the world has seen changes in so many different areas. Privacy no longer exists. We now live in a world that has gotten smaller and smaller. Our personal lives have become public. Some days, you feel like you cannot even sneeze without somebody on the other side of the world knowing about it.

I grew up as a child of the 1980s. I grew up in a time where rotary phones we're starting to be replaced by cordless phones. I remember a day in 1987, when my parents bought a microwave for the first time. I was just a kid, but I remember thinking about how exciting it would be to be able to cook food without having to use the stove! The world was changing so fast.

I remember a day in 1992, when my uncle came over to our house and brought along with him a cellular phone. It was the size of a small watermelon. He took great pleasure in showing it off and I remember thinking to myself about the day that would come when I would own my own cellular phone.

By the time I got to high school, Internet dating had become a thing. People were using the Internet to meet potential life partners. I remember profiles we're so private and people would safeguard their personal information. Even to this day, dating websites are full of profile names and safely guarded information so that the people using those sites can feel safe. I never thought it would get further than that, meaning that even though people were putting their pictures online and writing profiles, I never thought it would get to the point where people would put their full personal information online.

By the time I finished college, there was more sharing of personal information online. Social media had yet to arrive, but the writing was on the wall. This was the early 2000's. At this point, a person could use search engines online to look up information on individuals, even though it was hard to find any information because those were considered the early days of the World Wide Web.

In the years leading up to the beginning of Social Media, there were websites around where people did share personal information, to a point. People would go on websites such as Nexopia and Myspace, and on those websites, younger people would network with each other and meet each other potentially. These were not dating websites; they were merely websites that younger generation people used in order to connect with each other.

Then came Facebook. It was not until March of 2007 that I first created my Facebook account. In fact, many people in my circle of influence began using Facebook in the year 2007. I couldn't believe the invasion of privacy that it showed, and I especially did not think that its popularity would last. I totally thought that people would eventually get sick of their privacy being invaded and would lose interest. Boy was I wrong.

Suddenly, there was this website where everybody was putting their personal information, and every day I would add new friends, people that I've known my entire life. I watched people post private pictures, share private information, and make stupid posts (Including myself). I did not know what to make of this, but I decided to get on the train with everyone else.

Growing up, I never thought we would live in a world where privacy does not exist. Even to this day, I open any one of my social media accounts, and I see something that surprises me. These days, people post anything and everything. If they break a nail, they post it. If they achieve their goals, they post it. If somebody passes away, they post it.

In some instances, such as remembering somebody close to us that passed away, it's good to share their memory with the world. Situations such as this, is what's right about social media in the world today. The reason I say this, is that it can help heal. Achieving your goals is another great example. If there is a way you can inspire others, then do it.

Negative posts, the world can do without, but that's a part of life too. I can give all sorts of examples of positive posts and negative posts, to be honest, that would take at least 100 books to cover. The world of social media is now upon us and it will continue to be part of the fabric of our lives forever.

Distinguishing between what's real and what's fake, however, is what I am trying to do now. You cannot always believe what you see on Social Media. As real as our world is, it can be just as fake. What we see today on our feeds, is likely the exact opposite of the truth. They say that the truth will set you free, but at the same time, we lie to ourselves every day.

The Unreal world of Social Media is just that, unreal. My position is quite simple, if you let it get to you, it will be nothing but fake. It will be nothing but phony. There's a much greater world outside of the world of Social Media, but future generations might not see that, as they will grow up in the age of just that, social media.

TABLE OF CONTENTS

INTRODUCTION   3

SECTION 1 - THE BEGINNING   11

CHAPTER 1 - THE LEAD UP   13

CHAPTER 2 - THE EVOLUTION   19

CHAPTER 3 - INITIAL ISSUES   25

CHAPTER 4 - INVASION OF PRIVACY   31

CHAPTER 5 – NON-USERS OF SOCIAL MEDIA   37

CHAPTER 6 - RELATIONSHIP STATUS   43

CHAPTER 7 - RELATIONSHIP KILLER   47

CHAPTER 8 - THE EARLY SPAMMERS   53

CHAPTER 9 - IRRESPONSIBLE POSTS   59

CHAPTER 10 - ALBUMS TO REAL-TIME POSTS   65

SECTION 2 - BECOMING CULTURE   69

CHAPTER 11 - 2007   71

CHAPTER 12 - 2008   77

CHAPTER 13 - 2009   81

CHAPTER 14 - 2010   85

CHAPTER 15 - 2011   91

CHAPTER 16 - 2012   95

CHAPTER 17 - 2013   101

CHAPTER 18 - 2014   105

CHAPTER 19 - 2015   109

CHAPTER 20 - 2016   115

SECTION 3 - THE FUTURE   **119**

CHAPTER 21 - CELEBRITY PARTICIPATION   121

CHAPTER 22 – INFLUENCERS   127

CHAPTER 23 - GOING LIVE   131

CHAPTER 24 - FACEBOOK   135

CHAPTER 25 - TWITTER   141

CHAPTER 26 - INSTAGRAM   147

CHAPTER 27 - SNAPCHAT   151

CHAPTER 28 - TIK TOK   157

CHAPTER 29 - THE CLASS OF 2025   161

CHAPTER 30 - THE LONG TERM EFFECTS   169

CONCLUSION   175

GENERAL MODERN TERMS   179

SECTION 1

THE BEGINNING

CHAPTER 1

THE LEAD UP

How did we get to this point? It's true, the world is getting smaller. There's no question about that. But how is it that privacy has gone out the window? It's almost like 99% of the world just does not care anymore, they post everything. Are we that bored? Maybe. The world is constantly changing, and Social Media is now a big part of it.

I guess we should have seen this coming from the day Windows 95 hit the market. The World Wide Web came into mainstream life, and the rest is history. Just like the 1950s, where many homes were starting to get television sets, by the 1990s, every home was starting to get personal computers.

The fact that you could now go online, and search information was out of this world. 'Surfing the web' was a term used constantly in the late 1990s. I'd sit home and watch celebrity interviews on television and when asked about their hobbies, sure enough, 'surfing the web' came up!

Before, you needed to pick up a phone book to find a phone number, little things like ordering pizza became easier. By this time, you could go online and not only order your pizza, but you could even look at the menu! This might sound a bit strange now, how I am referring to this, but trust me, at that time, it was a revolution.

Growing up, the most exciting thing I did on the computer was playing 'The Oregon Trail.' That was at school mind you, as in the 1980s, I didn't live in a home that had a personal computer. For those of you old enough, you know which game I am talking about. You may have even played it yourself!

Businesses started having presence online, and even back then it was widely known that the future of business was online. If you did not have a presence online, then you were in danger of falling behind the times. It was no joke, even people from the 'old school' had to suck it up and get with the changes coming to market.

Governments did their best to regulate what was being put online. The internet that you see today is vastly different from the 1990s. These days, there is unlimited forms material online that is 'not suitable for younger audiences.' Anything and everything can be found on there, news, sports, adult sites, etc.

As the internet started to evolve more into the mainstream, society as whole started to become more comfortable with the internet, and thus more and more people felt comfortable with what was being put online, and they became more comfortable with what they were putting online.

I honestly do not believe that Facebook would not have worked in the 1980s. In fact, Mark Zuckerberg may have been jailed for creating a platform like this. It's hard to truly know how it would have been received 20 years earlier, But I can tell you with the utmost certainty that his roadblocks would have been 100 times more difficult. I will not take anything away from his creation, because it did change the world, but his timing was better.

Society was not ready for something like this in the 1980s. People were more than happy enjoying their new microwaves. The roadblocks that Mark Zuckerberg encountered in present day were hard enough. But the government of years past would have shut him down. Someone like that, with that much drive, would have found a way through it, but in a much lengthier time frame.

The writing was on the wall from the very beginning. Once it got to the point where anyone can create whatever they want to post online, such as creating their own websites in the beginning, then we almost knew it would go further. Many people, including myself, did not want to believe it, not at all. I did not want the entire world knowing my personal business.

I remember my grade 6 teacher telling us that computers may someday run the world. Well, it has now become reality. Take a walk down the street, down any street, in any country, in any part of the world. You will see at least 50% of the people walking and looking down at their phones. At 50%, I am being very conservative. The next time you are out, look around you, computers do run the world now, as everyone is driven by their phone.

The world was destined to get to this point, the sharing of private information on a public platform. It was inevitable. As the world continues to evolve, we will continue to see society adopting a more relaxed approach to privacy. I just hope we do not see people walking around naked in 20 years because the world decides to become more accepting of public nudity. Then again, who knows?

CHAPTER 2

THE EVOLUTION

The basic parts of Social Media have always stayed the same. Connecting with friends, posting about life, and general good overall vibes. The evolution really is in the options that each medium provides. From Facebook to Twitter, from Instagram to Snap Chat, and now mediums like Tik Tok. They all have the basic same general idea, and they continue to evolve as well.

It all started with people posting pictures, albums after weekends of fun. They would take photos during their time having fun, then the next morning they would post the pics from the night before. There was not much 'real time' in the early days of social media. This was the era before 'Apps' and people were not accessing internet on their phones yet. Well, really it was at the beginning of the 'Internet on your phone' era.

As more and more people started accessing internet on their phone, Twitter was created and really pushed the 'real time' posts. People were able to post pictures of their fun nights, all while out having fun at the same time! This eliminated the wonderful Sunday mornings we would have during 2007 when you would wake up and see idiotic posts. We will get more into this later, as it is a juicy topic. Yum.

Instagram then came along and is basically a version of Twitter that younger people use. You can post pictures at first, along with a worded post that was not limited, as it was on Twitter. Obviously, the profile name could be whatever you want it to be, so it gave a level of privacy that Facebook could not give. Basically, it allowed people to post more provocative pictures while maintaining some level of privacy if you could call it that.

Snap Chat then came along and provided more privacy, as people would post 'real time' videos of their lives. The great thing about this medium is that videos and pictures could only be viewed once or twice, and then it would go away forever. On top of that, if someone screenshotted your post, you would know. Snap Chat has also provided a way of communication that is utilized just as much as your phone. When people meet these days, they exchange Snap Chat handles instead of phone numbers. Mind you, this refers to the younger generation.

The evolution of Social Media is ongoing and will continue to be that way. It seems that there is more of a push toward more privacy really, in terms of profile names, but still people are broadcasting their personal lives constantly, that just will not change.

When people get emotional, man oh man, that is when the doozies come out. No matter how many times people make irresponsible posts, they tend to do it again and again. Having the power of that phone in your hands, with a camera installed, anyone can lash out at the world at any time. If they are drunk, if they are high on drugs, or even if their boyfriend/girlfriend dumped them. Human beings are known to say and do stupid things when emotions get involved.

Like it or not, everyone has a story of the time they made a stupid post that made them look like an idiot, we are all guilty of that. The evolution of Social Media is designed to protect people from embarrassing situations like that. That is the reason for using profile names. That is also the reason you can block or restrict people. Having that ability makes people a lot more comfortable with signing up.

In the early days of Social Media, I had a friend of mine that was in a relationship with a beautiful girl. She was out of his league and he knew it (Kind of a negative attitude to have). He was the jealous type as well, and this did not get received well on her end. He acted like a complete jackass every time he saw another guy put a comment on one of her posts. By the way, that is not a particularly good way to build trust with a girl if you are a guy and you act like that, just saying.

Anyways, she got so fed up that she put him on restricted profile. This really shook him up. I was a little bit in disbelief watching him suffer, I have always held my emotions well, but this guy was a mess. In retaliation, he decided to put her on restricted profile. LMFAO, yeah, like that was going to work. Please keep in mind, it's easy to laugh at now, but at the time I did my best to be supportive. This was still all new to all of us.

This guy clearly acted in a very immature way throughout the entire process, so he got what was coming to him in a way. A few days later, she blocked his ass on Facebook. This was not good. He was in tears, believe it or not. A few of us were with him as he tried calling her, but to no avail. He ended up getting black-out drunk that night. I am not sure exactly what he did once he woke up, I assume he called her off the hook. I assume this because she dumped his ass the next day.

This was my first experience watching someone come unglued at the hands of watching their significant other get attention on Social Media, and it would not be the last.

CHAPTER 3
INITIAL ISSUES

I have been chomping at the bit waiting to get to this chapter! As I have already mentioned, Sunday mornings in the beginning were a lot of fun. You just never knew what you would wake up to when you woke up and saw the posts from the night before. In the early days, Facebook was accessed from laptops and desktops computers mostly. I remember waking up on Sunday mornings, logging in, and seeing people with 'strange' statuses. Some examples included the following.

1) 'I like screaming my own name during sex!'
2) 'My life goal is to sleep with every guy, and girl, in this town.'
3) 'I'm an idiot.'

4)   'I enjoy eating feces.'
5)   'Hey guys, I was actually Elvis in my previous life, just saying.'
6)   'Please punch me the next time you see me.'
7)   'Addicted to Viagra'
8)   'In need of a good spanking!'
9)   'In my spare time, I enjoy covering myself up with peanut butter and frolicking in a bathtub filled with jelly.'
10) 'I'm secretly into diaper bondage.'

There's no shame in doing the things or being involved in any of the above scenarios if it doesn't compromise your health. I have nothing against anyone who is into any of the above. To each, their own. But these examples show exactly what I am talking about. The initial issues of Social Media posts.

It was simple, people would go out on weekends, have a great time, and indulge in some sort of alcoholic or drug induced state. If they were not already at someone's home, possibly a house party, they would invariably make their way to someone's home for the 'after party.' Now this is where the real drama begins.

In the mid-2000s, most homes in the first world had a personal, desktop computer. These days, not so much, only when someone has a home office. Back then, these desktop computers were accessible to most visitors. So, when you involved partying, alcohol, or drugs, you were sure to get some irresponsibility.

A targeted person would be someone that was under the influence, and then have a wonderful idea to go on the desktop and sign in! We all know how chaotic house parties can be, so at some point, that targeted person would leave that profile open and rejoin the festivities of the party. This made for easy prey.

Once that person passed out, someone else at the party would go to open their profile and see that the previous person did not sign out. Bingo! This person would be licking their chops thinking about all the sorts of stupid posts they could put. Meanwhile, the targeted person would wake up the next day, hungover, to a call from a friend asking if that post was true! Their next post was usually either an explanatory post or just a simple 'fuck you' directed at the person who did it.

I personally remember a post from a good friend of mine, he had come out as gay. It was quite a long post with him explaining how he loved everyone, and he was not sure how everyone would take it. Unfortunately, I am sure he did lose some friends over that and that is just too bad, because he was always a great person, still is.

He was a manager at a local restaurant/bar, and I ran into him a few months later. It was loud and we did not have much time to talk, but I did offer him my support. He gave me a strange look, and I think it had something to do with the fact that others did not receive him well after coming out. Before walking away, I gave him a big kiss on the cheek, the look he then gave me was even more strange. I am not gay, but I do have gay friends, and I am very proud to call them my friends because they stood up and had the courage to be who they are in a world that is not always accepting. I figured he was just surprised at my offer of support and left it at that. That night was the last time I had ever seen him in person, to this day.

Fast forward, some 5 years later, I was out with some friends when I met a woman in a restaurant that I absolutely had to talk to. I simply walked over to her table and struck up a conversation. She received me well and we had a great talk. Then she told me that she had been working at the same restaurant/bar that my friend had managed, and she had been there for the last 6 years! I asked her about him, and sure enough, they were great friends. I then proceeded to tell her the story of when he first came out of the closet. This was when things got bizarre.

She got noticeably quiet and just stared at me. After what seemed like an eternity, she finally spoke again. "He's not gay. He is actually engaged to be married." I was so taken off guard I responded to her with a very stupid question. "To a woman?" Yeah, I know, very stupid, right?

As it turned out, all those years earlier, he was a victim of passing out somewhere, and somebody else going into his profile and 'updating' his status. I personally think all of that is very childish, but that was the world we were living in at that time. To this day, I have not run into him at all, but if I ever do, I am sure we will have an honest laugh at the entire misunderstanding. Don't worry guys, I won't kiss him this time, I'm sure his wife wouldn't like that.

This was the first time I had realized what the world of Social Media was all about, that you cannot believe everything you see on there. This situation foreshadowed what was to eventually come as the world of Social Media evolved. At first, it seemed very real, everyone looked so happy. No confusion.

Other issues in the early days included all the misunderstandings that came along with it. As it was new to everyone, the experiences that we were having, well the world was just not ready for this. I surely was not ready for it, nobody was.

CHAPTER 4

INVASION OF PRIVACY

Is there privacy anymore? Privacy used to be the ability of someone to seclude or hide information from others and keep it to themselves. Things in life that are considered private can be provided on a long list. Your family life, where you live, how much money you make, and the list goes on. This does not exist anymore.

When something is private to someone, it means that it is something they should prefer to keep to themselves, like a secret almost. It provides people with a sense of security knowing that their private matters remain their own. This was a major problem back at the beginning of the Social Media era, as many people were just not ready to let the world in.

These days, it feels like you can not even use the bathroom without the whole world knowing about it. This just shows you what has become of the world today. Not only is privacy gone out the window, but the speed at which news becomes public travels at the speed of lightning.

Back in 1996, when the greatest rapper of all time, Tupac Shakur was killed, within a week, everyone was talking about it. I didn't believe it; I did not want to believe it. I was not even a fan of rap at the time. A lot of people did not want to believe it, but it was true. The world was talking about it a week later.

By 1997, Princess Diana passed away and the next day, it was world news. It did travel fast, and the world was changing rapidly already. At that time, the world wide web was in full swing mode and taking over, so news was travelling faster than ever.

In 2009, after the beginning of Social Media, Michael Jackson met his demise. He passed away in the afternoon and headlines around the world that night showed the unfortunate news. This was the first time in history that the whole world was brought news of a celebrity death so quickly. That was until 2020, Kobe.

In 2020, Kobe Bryant, one of the greatest basketball players in history, and likely one of the 10 most recognizable faces on the planet, died in a helicopter crash. Within one hour of that helicopter hitting the ground, the entire world knew. That was it, this is the new world we live in.

Over the years, Social Media platforms have been susceptible to breaches of privacy and attacks on their systems. Every so often we read a story in the news of how some company was hacked or breached in some way, and millions of users' private information was compromised. Companies such as Facebook have faced endless scrutiny from governments all around the world for privacy issues. And yet, millions of people worldwide continue to use these platforms, happily providing their information.

I remember back then; people were calling it 'crack book.' This was a direct play on the fact that Facebook was so addicting, it was basically like a drug. Anyone that knows anything about addiction or has been close to someone who had issues of addiction, they know that people couldn't care less about issues of privacy. If they want to log on, they will log on.

I hosted a party in mid-2007 and the next day I posted pictures of the event. One of my employees called me the next day and asked me to take down a picture that showed her draped all over another guy, a guy that was not her boyfriend. Apparently, the boyfriend saw this picture and freaked out. You cannot go anywhere anymore without people knowing.

Everyone has their vices; everyone has their secrets. Suddenly, we were seeing into the personal lives of people we know, and people we do not know. Out of the woodwork came all the gamblers, the playboys, and the criminals. People were posting pictures every week and they were getting a clear vantage point of what their 'online' friends now looked like. Being a criminal just got tougher, but that's not so bad.

It became harder to cheat, that's not so bad either. The bigger problem for people overall was that they could not do the things they normally do, without everyone knowing. There are the people, even to this day, who have avoided Social Media altogether. We will get into this in the next chapter. Everyone has something to hide, or basically something they do not want to share with the world, but at what cost are they willing to compromise?

It is just a plain fact that privacy in this modern world means something different than it did 50 years ago. The evolution of Social Media has allowed for people to guard themselves better when they open profiles and start posting. At the same time, nothing can hide the fact that you are posting pictures and videos of your private life. The new world has arrived.

CHAPTER 5

NON-USE OF SOCIAL MEDIA

Behold anyone that you know who does not use Social Media. Do those people even exist? In my personal life, I have met hundreds, if not, thousands of people through various business projects and personal activities. I can say with the utmost certainty that the amount of people I have known in my life that do not use Social Media whatsoever... well I can count on one hand.

At first, there were many people who held out and did not want to succumb to the 'desire' of Social Media. You would see posts containing 5 people, with 4 people clearly tagged and making comments. What stood out, however, was that one person who was not tagged, was not writing comments below, and overall, they did not have a profile.

These people were of all backgrounds, it was not one segment of the population. Some of these people were just private, straight up. Others had massive egos and they figured they were 'above' falling into the Social Media Trap. Taking it one step further, some people had a lot to hide, such as having multiple intimate partners. There were many people that had all sorts of reasons why they held out, but the truth is, many of these people did succumb to the desires of Social Media and signed up eventually.

To this day, however, there still is that small segment of the first world population that will never fall into it. They just have no interest, and to be honest, I do not blame them. It's all fake anyways, all the happy posts and pictures, bullshit. Professional wrestling is more real than Social Media sometimes.

One might ask the question, 'How do these people operate in the modern world?' They just do, plain and simple. They have made a point in their lives to live as they want, without the added dramatics that Social Media can bring into their world. It will always be like that, even in the future when kids that were born into the Social

Media era grow up. There will always be that small segment of the population that does not give a flying fuck.

If you can pinpoint one of these people in your life today, you can ask them all sorts of questions. They will tell you to your face that they can do without looking at other people's lives on Social Media every day. They don't care if you broke a nail, they don't care if you ate McDonald's for dinner, they don't care if you bought a new car, they don't care if you got married, they don't care if you went on vacation, they don't care if you achieved a lifetime goal, they don't care if you bought a new shirt, they don't care if you took a shower this morning (Unless you are seeing them in person at some point today), they don't care how much money you make, and last, but not least, they don't care about you.

It has been said that people who spend less time on Social Media are more successful in life overall. That is because they are not wasting their time going through hundreds of posts putting likes and posting comments. That does make sense regarding the successful limited users, but on the other hand, it has become part of the fabric of society in today's world.

The people that do not indulge in the use of Social Media are truly not missing out on anything. It is their life, and if they do not want to engage, that's their prerogative. I am sure many of them have dabbled at some point, or at the very least, it has crossed their mind. It is just like anything else in life, if you do not want to get on the boat, then you just don't.

I personally know a guy who has held out from the very beginning, he still does. He happens to be a phenomenally successful person in his industry, an incredibly powerful executive. In all the years I had known him, we only discussed the topic one time. His stance was quite simple, he enjoys his life to the fullest. He is very private; at the same time, he makes a lot of money. With that money, he uses it to live his life at full capacity, with travel and finer things as well, beautiful women, nice cars, and expensive clothing.

He prefers not to rub his success in the face of others. He has his own circle, and he is happy with that. He does not want 'vultures' in his circle. That meaning, he does not want people getting close to him with the sole purpose of taking advantage. Nobody around him knows how much money he makes or has, but I can guarantee it's well into the 7 figures.

People like that have a specific purpose. They want to maintain their privacy so as not to put themselves into a situation that would compromise their current standing, either monetarily, physically, mentally, or even emotionally. That last one, emotionally, could be the ball breaker for real. He told me himself, if he gets involved with the wrong woman, one who just goes after him for money, as he told me in his words, he would be 'fucked.'

CHAPTER 6
RELATIONSHIP STATUS

Back in the day, what did it mean to become 'Facebook Official? People did take it seriously at first. That is, until all the drama started. People were not conditioned to the fact that it takes two to tango. I will explain by using a prime example.

One day at work, I got into a conversation with a girl that worked with me. She was very pretty, and I could tell that she had no problem gaining attention of men in general. However, this day, she was not just upset, she was pissed off. Apparently, a guy she was on and off with posted that he was in a relationship with her, without her having knowledge about it until she logged on.

At that point, both sides did have to accept their statuses so that it would become public, but this idiot took it one step further. He posted a picture of them together and commented about how 'in love' he was with his 'girlfriend.' Firstly, he updated his own status, and while he was waiting for her to make things official, he jumped the gun and posted that picture. Foolish.

Once people started to get more understanding of how their circle of friends reacted to such things, they started being careful as to what they post, especially the relationship status. In a relationship, there is always one of the parties that wants to keep things low key, so being the person that jumps the gun, it is never a good position to be in.

Some people, unbelievably, never learn. I knew a guy that was a Facebook friend of mine in recent years, and he posted EVERYTHING. Anytime he posted something, the comment threads below his pictures would be massive, and he loved every minute of it. I would run into him from time to time in real life and we would exchange pleasantries.

One day, this guy gets himself a new girlfriend, and this was when he became the 'Post King' in my estimation. He was smitten with this new lady and he was posting all sorts of fun and goofy pictures with her. I was happy for him, just like everyone else. This guy had met the girl of his dreams, it is a beautiful story… or is it?

3 months later I ran into him at a local supermarket and I asked him how things were going with the woman. He seemed a bit uncomfortable with the question and he answered me in such a way that he needed a break and did not want to lose his 'freedom.'

I wasn't buying it. I knew something was up, so I pushed him a bit more. He finally relented and told me that she dumped his ass. He then went on to tell me that the minute he changed his Facebook status to 'in a relationship' with this woman, well that was the beginning of the end. After that, she felt smothered by his constant posts and the added pressure of being this perfect woman to all his friends.

This was very upsetting to hear, and I could tell it bothered him. I never realized that there was an added pressure when changing the relationship status on Facebook, but I guess there is. One last thing, he told me that he kept running into people and they would ask him about how things were going with her, and he simply got tired of answering the same questions repeatedly. I was wondering why the posts had stopped.

He said he wouldn't make that mistake again, and the next girl he would date, he would make sure not to post anything until they were together at least 6 months. Well he never stayed on course with that, because not even a month later, he found a new 'soulmate' and started posting with her. Can you guess what the result was there? Yup, she dumped his ass too.

I have been dumped before, many times, but never for doing something this stupid. This story, however, does lead into the next chapter, which is about the 'relationship killer.' Be careful when you start to become official online, the moral of these stories I have shared is simple. If you want to make things official, make sure the other person feels the same way about you, and don't over do it!

CHAPTER 7

RELATIONSHIP KILLER

Social Media has long been blamed for killing relationships worldwide. It has become an unfortunate by-product of this phenomenon. Everyone seems to have story of a time when they posted something that led to the breakup of their relationship. This held true especially in the first few years of Social Media.

As stated previously, the general public were not yet conditioned to handle situations where irresponsible pictures and posts turned up online. The world was not yet ready, and the general public paid a heavy price. It cost many people one of the few things that money can not buy, love.

I remember a friend of mine was dealing with this exact issue, he and his girlfriend broke up due to the excessive fights they had, which were all caused by their use of social media! They both were extremely jealous people, and once they started seeing how many 'opposite sex' friends each other had, it drove them nuts!

Every time they would be out, one of them would make a reference to it, and then bam! The war was on. You may find it a bit strange reading this now and seeing how immature some people could be, but trust me, this was normal back then. People often broke up over Social Media posts. Welcome to the new world ladies and gentlemen.

The content of the pictures and posts became another source of ire for people that were already in dramatic relationships. The posting of new albums, and the subsequent comments or threads that formed after. Watching your boyfriend or girlfriend flirt with someone else on a thread, in front of the entire world, was blasphemous! They had to be punished! Well they were not punished, in fact they were just dumped, only to resurface once again after relenting and taking down the post. Sometimes, I can't believe I am writing this stuff.

The dramatics that came with the new era of Social Media was just too much for some people, and they left the scene. However, these same people would resurface years later with a new lease on life, a new attitude, and likely freshly divorced. They would add friends like crazy and post non-stop. Good for them, because being saddled in a relationship with a controlling figure may not be the most ideal situation in life, but people get stuck.

There were also high numbers of people who discovered, through Social Media, that their significant other was cheating on them. This can truly hurt you. This can truly hurt anyone that is involved in a loving relationship, a relationship where they would absolutely die for the other person. Imagine opening your Facebook in 2007 and seeing a picture of another woman draped all over your boyfriend, or vice versa.

The absolute hurt and pain that this caused could be labeled as devastating in some circumstances, for real. How can you recover from an experience like that? You would have to be an extraordinarily strong person emotionally to get through it, but still, a person would feel the sting of that experience for a lifetime. Emotions can be very controlling at times.

You might be reading this book now thinking some of this stuff is crazy. If you were around during that era, however, you know exactly what I am talking about. This is real life and it can be harsh at times, but it just goes to show you how fragile the human spirit can be.

We can move now to the ugly D-word, divorce. These days, over 30% of divorces start as online affairs. It is so easy for immature, horny people to get to someone they want. It is a simple formula, add them, and then direct message them. Easy peasy. People like this are out to kill a current relationship because they have their own agenda. These are the most lethal relationship killers.

Before Social Media, we never had such easy access to one another. It is so easy to reach out to anyone now, just shoot them a direct message and you are off to the races. Think about this, a beautiful woman posts a picture of herself in a bikini, in 2007-2010. How many direct messages do you think she receives from horny guys on her friends list? I thought so.

I knew one girl whose boyfriend would go through her phone every night and send a 'fuck you' message to each guy who had direct messaged her that day. I don't know what sort of emotional problems this guy had, but clearly, he did not have the emotional will power to withstand the changes coming to the world. I don't know what became of them, I lost touch and they aren't on Social Media anymore. Maybe they are and they have me blocked, whatever. She was nice but I didn't care much for him. Good riddance.

If you let it, Social Media will kill your relationship, period. Rise above it and be mature. Life is too short to get caught up in the little things.

CHAPTER 8

THE EARLY SPAMMERS

I don't know who put out the memo, but the beginning of Social Media saw a rise of Pyramid Scheme people on Facebook. It was a strange time, every other day I would get a 'mass message' in my direct messenger from someone on my friends list asking me to come to a meeting and learn how to earn thousands of dollars starting with a simple $100 investment.

The mentality was simple, people would open a Facebook account, realize that they now had instant access to hundreds of people they knew, and they would go about sending tons of messages to their friends. They thought it was an easy way to get rich! Little did they know, it just pissed people off.

I remember one guy on my friends list started a group chat, he added in around 50 people, and then proceeded to start a chat about finance and wealth, eventually wanting the conversation to get to what he was selling. By the way, his day job was as a heavy-duty mechanic, so I'm not sure why suddenly he was a financial guru. But he fell into that trap.

Somebody on his friends list did the same thing, spamming everyone until they got some interest. Just so you all know, this kind of thing pissed people off back then too. Anyways, most of the people left the chat group, while a few others gave some 'parting shots' on their way out. This was quite common back then, not so much now.

Poking was another favourite pastime of these so-called early spammers. I don't care who you are, if you had a profile opened anywhere between 2007 to 2011, you had at least one friend who would just keep poking you! Once you poked back, they, in turn, would poke back immediately. Talk about annoying!

At first, the poke was fun. But after the first few months of it being on Facebook, it just turned into an annoying quantity that nobody cared about. This was quite common during the time when many people accessed their Facebook from their desktop or laptop. I always wondered what the point of these people was, sending endless pokes that had no meaning. Personally, I only used the poke a few times until the novelty wore off. After I got bored, I went back to my normal life.

Sometimes these things can get quite ridiculous. I remember in 2009 running into a guy that I went to school with. We got to chatting and it turned out that he was one of these 'serial pokers.' After greeting, his first question; "Hey! Why don't you poke me back?"

Ok. Once I realized that this wasn't a sexual advance, I took a second to take in that question, which I found completely stupid. He wasn't even joking, he was serious. It was almost as if I had insulted him by not responding to his poke. That was the beginning of my understanding that Social Media can really affect people that are super sensitive. We have all been there, we have all been somewhat hurt or affected by something we have seen on Social Media. Some people just take it a step further.

I promised this guy that I would poke him back the next time I log in. This way, I wouldn't have to hear about it anymore during our conversation, which didn't last too much longer by the way. So, the next day when I logged in, I poked him back. Then, not even 2 seconds later, he returned the poke! I was not having this. I deleted the friendship and went on about my day. Exciting I know.

One truly annoying type of spam, and I will call it spam, is the messaging that some people received, mostly women receiving, from idiots who created fake profiles and sent messages, just trying to be funny. Most people reading this have received these sorts of messages, some could have been labelled as threatening, but for the most part, annoying.

I could never see the point of people wanting to waste their time doing that sort of stuff, just to upset someone else. I could understand the pyramid scheme people sending messages, but these fake user account messages were plain immature. In many cases, it was an ex-boyfriend or ex-girlfriend out to get their revenge by tormenting the person that broke up with them.

Social Media spam can fall under a few different situations. The bottom line is that it is annoying and always will be. In recent years, the amount of spam in all cases has become less, when it comes to Social Media. It is still present. The advertisements will always be around. The

Facebook poke does still exist as of 2020, but it is hardly used. It is not used as extensively as before. Thankfully, the threatening spam messages are not as prevalent either, that is good. Spam, however, will always be spam, whether it pertains to food or Social Media. Some people like it, and some people don't.

CHAPTER 9

IRRESPONSABLE POSTS

Imagine opening one of your Social Media accounts today and you see a post of one of your friends... in bed with their partner. Yes, you heard that right. In bed, with their partner, an entire album of photos of them both, partially clothed, and in bed! Pictures of them under the covers, pictures of them kissing each other, and general pictures of their 'pillow talk moments.'

I remember opening my account one morning in 2008 and this is exactly what I saw. I was a bit turned off, like most people may have been, but that was just one example of the many posts you would see back then, reckless and irresponsible. Social Media was so fresh in our society at that point. This alone was one of the reasons that people would post irresponsibly. They did not yet have the experience or realize just how sensitive certain material could be. They had no idea of the potential damage a bad post can cause, not only to them, but to the people around them.

In the years since, the person whom I had on my friends list that made this post, I have seen them a few times. She is a female and it was her boyfriend who was taking all the pictures and selfies. The pictures showed that he was the one in control of the camera. I didn't know him from a hole in the ground, but I sure as hell didn't like him.

Even though it has been years since that post went up, (It has been taken down since) every time I run into her, I think about that post. That truly sucks because she is a great person and I would never judge her, or anyone for that matter, for something their boyfriend did. I know, it's not the end of the world, but this goes to show you the mentality of society back then compared to now. People are more guarded now because they understand that inappropriate posting can be hurtful.

These days, there are still people who just don't give a fuck what they post, but they usually keep it on more private platforms such as Snap Chat or Instagram. Facebook remains the most sensitive form of Social Media and the profile names are their actual real names! I do admire people that post whatever they feel like posting, I only hope they keep it appropriate to a degree and do so in such a way that won't hurt people close to them.

It is important to note that even though the type of irresponsible posts have changed, the mere fact that irresponsible posts still happen is truth. As a Writer and published Author, I fully understand the power of words and what they can do. The power of how they can help, heal, and hurt.

While we do not see as many people posting sensitive material through their pictures, we still do see a lot of hurtful words being spoken worldwide. A real example of this would be the subject of racism. There are many people that have their own opinion and they feel like people want to hear them.

This is true for people that want to make a positive change or support positive change. I applaud these individuals. But for people that thrive on making senseless, derogatory, and/or racist statements, there is no place in the Social Media world for them. There are those that may argue the right to free speech. They do have a point, but at the same time, these same people can stick it. Nobody wants to read that sort of shit anyways.

The evolution of irresponsible posts has come a long way, from dumb to dumber. I have been extremely fortunate in the fact that I have never had a Social Media friend on any of my accounts, to my knowledge, that has made discriminatory or racial remarks that has offended people. If that were the case, I would delete that person and cut ties completely.

I have no time in my life to waste on people that are out to hurt and belittle others. Life is too short. If anything, someone getting exposed due to their own irresponsible posting serves them right. People's true colours are revealed when they get emotional and it bites them in the ass when they insult the innocent.

We live in a world that is constantly changing. Sometimes, I wonder if we are changing for the best or the worst. People have more freedom than ever to post their thoughts to the world, that is our society today. With that freedom, however, comes responsibility. At the tip of our fingers, we hold the power to communicate our thoughts and feelings to the world. With this, we need to be aware of this power which we possess and keep it for positive instead of negative.

I cannot leave this topic without referring to one last situational point. People posting long rants directed at their exes. This is by far the most common type of negative posting that exists in the world today. You can always tell if someone has gone through some sort of drama when they make a dramatic post about relationships. They mention that they are posting for the good of conveying the message, but they are truly posting so that their ex can see it. This sounds a bit immature, but it is common. In the years to come, we will keep seeing more irresponsible posts, it's inevitable, just ponder before you post.

CHAPTER 10

ALBUMS TO REAL TIME

In the first 6 months of life on Social Media, it was all about posting the photo albums. It seemed like a race amongst people, to take a ton of pictures on the weekend, and then post them by Sunday or Monday so that everyone could see what a great life they were living. I even had one friend, by the end of 2007, that had over 200 albums posted!

Remember, a lot of people were still accessing Social Media through their desktops and laptops, not their phones. Interestingly, a hot commodity were those USB cables that everyone was using to upload their pictures from their phones to their computers. Every time you went to a party, someone would ask if you had a USB cable.

As you can see, with the rapid changes we are seeing in technology, uploading full albums has become a thing of the past. These days, people just post real time pictures or videos when they are out and about, enjoying their lives. The shear horror of having a ruptured USB cable on a Sunday morning has become a thing of the past.

Everyone now is posting their lives, up to the minute, and it is fantastic. Anyone posting pictures from previous days is clearly behind the ball in terms of modern era Social Media posting. The very minute something is happening, it is being posted. So, everyone in your circle knows what is going on in your life up until right now!

Speaking of what is going on in the present, how about going live? Posting live videos, when it came out, the most extreme of Social Media users were excited to try this new medium of communication. The biggest risk that many people saw was that sometimes, you could not fully control the material.

Think about this, when people post, they always want to show their best 'side or angle.' Going live takes all the preparation out of the scenario and it exposes people to having to show all their cards in the truest sense of the word. If you are going live and your hair isn't done the way you like, or if you still have food on your face from lunch earlier, I will say this. Going live don't lie, straight up.

In this world, everything needs to be current, up to the second, and right now, that's it. The world has become so small and bored to some people, reading yesterday's news just won't cut it. I think it is fun to 'go live.' There is nothing wrong with a little bit of unknown. Nothing at all.

SECTION 2

BECOMING CULTURE

CHAPTER 11
2007

We can say this about any year, that it was a year that changed the world. But in the world of Social Media, 2007 was that year. Personally, I joined up in 2007, along with millions of people worldwide. Even though Facebook was founded in 2004, it wasn't until 2007 when it hit the mainstream in a big way. It was making headlines all over the world, and everyone was talking about it. In fact, you didn't have to go far to find a conversation about it. Forget water cooler talk, this thing was bigger than life!

I can very clearly remember the day I first joined up. I was at work when a fellow employee of mine called me to her desk and asked me if I have Facebook, so she can add me. I told her I'd never heard of it and I wasn't interested. She then opened her profile on her desktop to show me. I was not overly impressed. Then she opened a profile of one of her friends, a gorgeous, jet black haired, olive skin beauty. Her profile picture was of her wearing a 2-piece bikini. And well... I am a guy, so I dropped everything and created my own profile.

Go ahead and laugh at me all you want. The fact is that most men at that time only joined so that they can get closer to women, or a woman that was in their circle. Anyone that tells you different is lying. There's nothing wrong with that, but fact is fact. Many women I interviewed said they originally joined so that they could communicate and share pictures with their friends more easily. Men just happened to follow them.

Those first few months were exciting! Every day I would add new friends, people I hadn't seen in years. I would send messages showing my excitement that they'd discovered this new platform as well! At the same time, people that were holding out, were crumbling and giving in, one by one. Almost every week I would see a post that would read something like this; "So I finally gave in and got Facebook. Add me guys!"

This phenomenon swept the entire globe like a bolt of lightning. It was that fast, honestly it was. The creator, Mark Zuckerberg, rocketed to fame in a mere matter of months. By the following year, it had over 100 million users. By 2020, Facebook had nearly 3 billion users across its platforms, Facebook, Instagram, WhatsApp, and Messenger. That's how big this is.

Media companies jumped all over this right from the start. Advertising, the right kind, can do wonders for any company. They realized that since so many people started using Facebook, it was an excellent opportunity to target specific audiences. Marketing on Social Media was relatively new back then, but well received.

The world was still getting used to all of this so there was a lot of trial and error in advertising. Advertising on Social Media, however, was bound to become successful because that's where everyone was. Go to where the people are, the masses, and you will surely find your market within.

These days, there are a lot of sponsored ads which are generally presented in a non-invasive way. Instead of being blown in your face, they are put in front of you, usually with the option of 'swiping up' or 'opening' the link. Short and sweet is the name of the game, doing just enough to gain the audience attention before they change the channel.

2007 was also interesting in the fact that it was the start of the Global Financial Crisis. I honestly don't think there was any correlation between the crisis and the sudden rise of Social Media. It was Definitely a time of change. Towards the end of 2007 was when we started seeing the posts regarding the crisis.

Since personal information was just starting to become public, as we have covered in different areas of this book already, I would see posts of all sorts hit the feeds. A lot of people were in financial trouble and their posts clearly reflected that for sure.

I had a friend who posted about losing his home outside of Detroit, Michigan. He was going to fight to keep his $250,000 house which only had $140,000 left on the mortgage. He was planning on losing some equity, but he figured there was enough to sustain the meltdown. The next day, he posted a picture of his house and the house next door. Both houses looked remarkably similar in size and condition. The house next door foreclosed and sold for $40,000.

To say this guy was upset is an understatement. His post showed his frustration and he was more than willing to share it with the world. This was the first time I had seen a post regarding the loss of money. When it comes to money, people are always a bit guarded. For instance, take a compulsive gambler. Gamblers have no problem talking about the bets they win, but they rarely talk about the bets they lose. That only happens once they've gotten some help or gotten into a support group.

As of 2007, all bets were off, no pun intended. Clean laundry as well as dirty laundry were now starting to be shown to the public on equal footing, to an extent. Going forward, the world would never be the same.

CHAPTER 12

2008

Since Facebook was still mostly being used off desktops and laptops, 'Facebook Chat' was developed and introduced, and it was fun! You could open several chats at once, all while browsing through your profile and feeds. I thought this was fantastic, and I indulged in it as well.

This was 3 years before messenger, which is much better equipped for your phone. The original 'DMs' started with Facebook Chat and everyone seemed to enjoy having multiple conversations at a time using their computer. Because it was so new, everyone who was logged in would usually respond. In the present day, many direct messages go unanswered, with only close friends deciding if they want to communicate.

A guy is 2008 messaging that pretty girl would likely get a response at least 60% of the time if she were online at the same time. 10 years later, that same scenario would only yield a 5% response rate, and that is being very generous. This excitement eventually faded as well, but you can see how rapidly things were developing at that time.

By 2008, we were starting to see a lot of more personal posts, such as weddings and birth of babies. It was starting to be around long enough for people to have posted life events that led to more life events. Buying a house, getting engaged, getting married, and then, having children.

I personally did a lot of travelling in 2008 and I saw first-hand, how important Social Media was starting to become personal lives. In 3rd world countries, poor kids would go to internet cafes to access the internet, and they would spend what little money their parents gave them, to access those few precious minutes on Facebook. It was quite sad to see this, but it was and is reality.

The best part of this particular year was that it was still new enough for people to respect it. Yet it had been around long enough for people to try and understand it better. Making better use of Social Media is what I am talking about. Back then, people were not using Social Media to make their exes jealous or anything of that nature.

When I call it the 'Unreal World of Social Media,' I am talking about how fake it has become. Back then, this wasn't so. People were gradually getting used to the idea of having this as part of everyday life, so any thoughts of using it for devious purposes was not on the table yet.

Sometimes, I wish we could go back to the 2008 mentality, but with the technology we have today. In the online world, it just seemed as though people were more honest and less cruel. It's too bad that it has become that way now, less honest and crueler, because it just gives people a sour taste on life in general, on bad days that is.

CHAPTER 13
2009

The 'Like!' In this year, the 'Like' was introduced and to this day, it is one of the most powerful mediums that Social Media has created. It is so simple, yet it makes a definite impact for sure. It is a staple of Facebook, Instagram, Twitter and Tik Tok. Especially at first, millions of people around the world would race to get their posts and pictures up, just to see how many 'Likes' they would receive!

I was even on that bandwagon as well. I remember the first time I started to get likes on my photos, I was intrigued. It started out small, 5 likes here, maybe 8 likes there. Then one day I received 20 likes on one of my photos and I was happy. I was on top of the world and felt as though my popularity was increasing by the day,

20 likes! On that very same day, I showed this to a female friend of mine. After she enjoyed a good laugh at my expense, she informed me that she would normally receive hundreds of 'Likes' on her pictures.

I looked up her profile and she was not kidding! Her pictures had hundreds of likes. But, of course, she was stunningly beautiful and had plenty of pictures posted from her recent trip to Mexico. All her pictures were of her wearing a bikini. That's just not fair, I can't compete with that!

Men, in general, absolutely love looking at beautiful women. That's just the way it is. Putting a like on her picture is just a way of trying to get a little attention for the most part. To this day, millions of pictures are being posted daily, with millions of 'Likes' being added. I cannot tell you what the percentage is of which gender spends more time putting likes on pictures, but I can tell you that it can be addicting.

Waking up in the morning in modern times, the first thing people reach for is their phone. They then proceed to go through their profiles and feeds and put 'Likes' on all of the posts and pictures by their friends. It has just become second nature and is a show of support towards the friends on the platform.

Sometimes I like to have a little bit of fun with it and when I see a friend in real life, I let them know that I'll be sure to put likes on all of their pictures in the future. It is a great way to keep touch with people in your circle. I don't do it often myself, but I still do indulge in it to this day.

No matter what platform you are using to this day, many people still do live and die by the amount of 'Likes' they get on their material. It is a definite ego boost. It may seem a bit petty to some people, but hey, if you don't like it, then delete your profile. There's nothing wrong with wanting to get a few more 'Likes' on your material. The 1980s ended a long time ago.

CHAPTER 14
2010

'The Social Network' was released and it was awesome! When Hollywood gets involved, it means that the story is big, plain and simple. Unless you were Mark Zuckerberg himself, none of us will truly ever know what exactly went on behind closed doors, a movie can only depict so much.

My favourite scene was when he asked to be 'recognized' for his breach of security at Harvard. Most of us will never know if that happened in real life but man would I have loved to be in the room when and if he said that. It takes balls to do what this guy did. With all the doors shutting in his face, he still found a way to make it work.

As the movie trailer shows, there was still a lot of the world signing in through desktops and laptops in 2010. Just Google the trailer and you'll see for yourself. This practice, however, was shifting as more and more people were directly accessing Facebook from their phones. You see now how quickly things change in our world post-2000.

When I was in High School back in the 1990s, I originally thought of making up a website that was like what Facebook represented. I bet millions of people around the world thought the same way I did and had that idea as well. At that time, nobody would ever have thought that it would work. People posting private photos for the world to see, along with their names and contact information? It could never work! I was wrong.

By 2010, Social Media was into the mainstream for good, and by the time the movie came out, Facebook had over 500 million users worldwide. As part of the marketing campaign leading up to the release of the movie, there was a website they created www.500millionfriends.com It is now no longer in service of Facebook publicly. Of course, by 2020, there were nearly 3 billion users of Facebook worldwide. I guess they can't make a new website every time they hit a new milestone.

McDonalds always used to update their Golden Arches signs with a small blurb underneath, 'Over 1 Billion People Served' or something of that nature. That was a long time ago. Their signs now read 'Over 99 Billion Served.' I'm sure they are referring to their hamburgers. It is widely estimated that McDonalds has served over 300 billion hamburgers in its history. I, for one, can proudly say that I have personally contributed to about 1000 of those in my lifetime. ⏧

By 2010, people had stopped referring to Facebook as 'Crack book' and you started to hear stories of people meeting on Facebook, and then falling in love. Now this was nothing new by this point, as this was happening from the beginning, but it was just happening a lot more frequently now. I assume because it had now become socially acceptable.

Just one year earlier, I was emcee at a wedding for a couple that met on Facebook. The groom met a wonderful woman right at the beginning of 2007 and they hit it off. They had mutual friends, but never actually knew each other until they connected on there. It turned out they worked for different companies in the same building, so somehow through all the pictures posted and such, they found a way to connect in person.

Interestingly, the groom instructed me to not bring this up during my time on stage. They absolutely did not want anyone knowing that they met on Facebook. This sounds odd for me to say now, being that it has become almost a norm these days for people to meet on Social Media. But back then, it was not socially acceptable yet and they weren't comfortable sharing it with the world.

Fast forward to the following year, I attended another wedding in the summertime and to my surprise, this couple had met on Facebook and they celebrated the fact that they met on Facebook. Everyone that spoke that night made some sort of reference to it, and it was a great time. By the time the bride and groom went up to speak, I knew it was coming, and I realized at that moment that society had once again shifted.

2010 can be called a transitional year in terms of social acceptance and the extent that people were willing to go to in order to tell their stories. The first few years of Facebook in all was a series of 'trial and error' experiences for people as they tried to figure out the difference of right and wrong when determining what to post online and how much to share of their 'use' of Social Media.

For example, there are fans of professional wrestling, but they won't admit it publicly. It is a sort of guilty pleasure to them. Facebook was considered a guilty pleasure to a lot of people up until 2010, that's just calling a spade, a spade. It was funny to hear some reactions when talking to people in person.

"Oh, I don't use it very often at all. I don't even like it, I have better things to do with my time."

Meanwhile, the same person who would say something like this quote above, well the next day they would post a slew of pictures on their profile and proceed to write a full explanation for each picture. Not often huh?

CHAPTER 15

2011

With this year came the introduction of the 'Timeline.' This is also now known as your 'Wall.' A little more organized and once again, part of the evolution of Social Media. In a world where constant change is almost necessary, the world of Social Media is no different. Staying up to date with society and business is essential.

For a good example, you need to look no further than the fast food industry. If you walk into any major fast food major franchise restaurant in 1984, you will notice only a select few products on the menu. Going back to McDonalds, you had the Big Mac, Filet-O-Fish, Cheeseburger, Quarter-Pounder, French Fries, Happy Meal, Egg McMuffin, Breakfast Menu, Milkshakes, McRib, and Chicken McNuggets. That was pretty much it at that time in most McDonalds across the Globe.

Walk into that same McDonalds in 2020, and you will find a menu that is at least triple that size, at least. You can get salads, wraps, and smoothies among other items. The expansion of the menu is a part of doing business in modern day. Also, locations are renovated and upgraded every few years in order to stay as that, modern. Constant change is the way it is these days. Nobody wants to fall behind the competition, they need to actively keep improving.

The 'Timeline' was added as a feature to help modernize Facebook and create a more active way to stay organized with the real time posts that had now become the norm. Publicly, friends could now post on your timeline with things such as wishing you a happy birthday. To this day, every year now, my timeline is full of well wishes on my birthday.

It also made way for the creepers to better creep your profile. Instead of them going through your profile and albums after getting to your page, they could now just go to your page and scroll down. At this point, they could see all your latest posts and pictures without having to dig too deep.

Privacy features have now put more power in the hands of the users as they can now control which segment of their friends can view certain posts and pictures that are on their timeline. You can put anyone you like on restricted profile now, an ability that wasn't always provided in the early days of this.

The 'Timeline' also makes it easier for users themselves to go back through posts and pictures by source of date. You could already do this before when it was just albums, but it has mechanisms that make it easier to restrict who can see it.

On another note, Snap Chat was created in 2011, but it would be a couple of years until it really hit the bigtime. It offered a form of direct video and picture messages that only lasted 24 hours and can be viewed only in that time frame. Same thing for the posts, once they are gone, they are gone. We will get more into this later, as in 2011 Snap Chat did not have the impact it did compared to the years that followed.

I keep referencing back to evolution throughout this book because the overall timelines which are being discussed here fall right into the initial growth phase of Social Media. It's like a baby learning how to flip on their stomach, then to crawl, and finally, to walk. By 2011, we were walking.

CHAPTER 16

2012

Thankfully, the world did not end. There were more beginnings and it all started with Instagram! Facebook purchased Instagram in this year and added to their 'monopoly' of Social Media at that time. Interestingly, switching gears for a moment, Twitter was now becoming a worldwide force as well. By 2012, Twitter had more than 100 million monthly users. The world of Social Media was ever expanding.

Instagram did provide a more private way of sharing, as we all know, your profile name does not have to be your real name. I recall opening my first profile and wondering about what nickname I would use as my profile name. I decided to go through the site myself and look at other names, just to get some ideas.

At that time, many of my friends had their names or something close to their names. In other cases, there were people who used their first and middle names, leaving out their last names. This practice is still quite common today. For obvious reasons, people still want to maintain their level of privacy.

Instagram also gave people who weren't on Facebook an opportunity to post with some privacy attached to their handles. There were millions of people, people that didn't use Facebook, who decided to give Instagram a shot.

This was a very smart move on behalf of Facebook as they still wanted to attract a segment of the population that weren't tuning in to Facebook. This was a way for Facebook to gain more followers on one of their platforms. This was a way for Facebook to help corner the market, so to speak.

Now that we had a new, more private platform of Social Media, society was becoming more liberal with the posts being put out there. This was the start of the use of social media for the means of 'making an ex jealous.' Since a platform like Facebook was more personal, and many people had their close family and friends on there, a site like Instagram allowed people to be more selective on who they added, as well as maintain some privacy due to the type of posts they put out overall.

A female friend of mine was in an on/off relationship with a real piece of shit narcissistic guy around this time. Every time they had a fight or broke up, he would go out with other people and make a point of posting at least one picture with a different girl. His posts would read something like "Making new friends," or wording along those lines. My friend was always hurting every time one of these posts appeared, usually within 24 hours of a fight or breakup.

Seeing this was the first time I had been exposed to yet another shift in Social Media, the using of it to hurt other people's feelings. To this day, it is a tactic widely practiced worldwide. My friend showed me a couple of that guy's posts and I found it disappointing. Not only was this guy using Social Media to inflict punishment on her, he was using these other girls to do it! He never had any intention of dating these other girls, they were just pawns on his chess board.

Personally, I never saw any good in lowering myself to this level. It's one thing to go out and brag about your accomplishments, your friends and family would be happy for you and it keeps positive vibes. But to get to a point where one person is using it to emotionally harm another, that is just low, but that's life in the modern day.

Also, by this year, food posts were really starting to make a big splash. It was fantastic at first, and still is to this day! On Facebook, people were generally posting pictures of everyday life, themselves, friends, and family. But the Instagram platform allowed people to go outside the norm and start posting plates of food!

Steak, mashed potatoes, filet mignon, salads, cheesecake, pizza, burgers, pasta, fries, poutine, eggs, waffles, salmon, tuna, chicken, watermelon, apples, oranges, cinnamon buns, cookies, shepherd's pie, meat loaf, rice... Do you want me to continue?

Going out for dinner had a whole new meaning. Once the waiter or waitress brought the food, hold on! A photo needs to be taken first, to capture the beauty that we are about to indulge in. I remember going on a date that year (Don't worry I had more than one ⏾) and she grabbed my hand just as I was reaching for my burger, "Wait! I need to take a picture first!"

Once I realized that she wanted a picture of the food, and not us together, I got out of the way so that she was able to take a fine photo. I was kind of taken off guard a bit, but I remembered that this was the new world. I can't complain about these things, the world was changing, either I get on the bus, or I get left behind.

CHAPTER 17

2013

This was Instagram's year of takeoff. The younger generation were more in tune with using Instagram as opposed to Twitter, or even Facebook to some degree. Facebook was still king of the mountaintop, likely always will be. At the same time, because Instagram provided more privacy, it resonated a lot better. Comparing it to Twitter, which restricted the size of their posts, in terms of wording, the younger generation sided with Instagram due to less restrictions on that level.

Everywhere I went that year, people were talking about it. Even though it had been around since 2010, the Facebook takeover launched it into Superstardom. Before I even opened my first Instagram account, everyone was raving about it and telling me to sign up.

It's funny, a general water cooler conversation in 1985 would have probably gone something like the following.

1985

Person 1 – Hey did you watch that 'Live Aid' concert yesterday?

Person 2 – Yeah! It was amazing, Freddie Mercury, I can't say enough about him, he's brilliant!

Person 1 – He totally stole the show for sure. I'm sure someday they'll make a movie about him. They gotta put that performance in the movie.

Person 2 – First they would have to find someone to be able to duplicate that, and I don't think it will happen anytime soon.

Person 1 – Well, I have quenched my thirst, back to work.

Person 2 – Chat later.

General water cooler talk had drastically changed by 2013, as the world was changing rapidly by this point, people were still as simple as ever. Human behaviour doesn't ever really change, what we talk about, however, does.

2013

Person 1 – Hey did you see what Sindy posted on Instagram last night?

Person 2 – I did! But I didn't put a like on it.

Person 1 – How come?

Person 2 – Because she's so fake! I can't stand that bitch.

Person 1 – Then why are you guys friends on there?

Person 2 – Well, I've quenched my thirst, back to work. (Mic drop)

As you can see, the use of Social Media was not the only thing that started taking up people's time. Talking about Social Media, in 2013, was quite common. These days, not as much, but keep in mind that with the quick rise of Instagram at this point, people were still trying to understand it. And when people are trying to understand something, they want to talk about it.

By the time Instagram was putting their hold on planet earth, people were more prepared. 'Already seen it,' and I mean that with regards to the rise of Facebook. Instagram users were having the time of their lives posting whatever they wanted and keeping some level of privacy.

Things that were not socially acceptable in 2007, became socially acceptable in 2013. For example, more provocative posts were becoming the norm. With the added level of privacy, men were happy to post 'shirtless selfies,' and women were happy to post 'boudoir' photos. Evolution, ladies and gentlemen, evolution.

CHAPTER 18

2014

Fitness industry people really started to take this and run with it by now. Body builders and fitness competitors alike, worldwide, began creating Instagram pages focussed on their careers. They would give tips on exercise, nutrition, and supplements.

Previously, we did have access to this information from magazines and the internet. But the major difference was that we were getting this information from millions of sources. This was bonus because anyone could now go on Instagram and find the information they need, and tailor it to their own life specifications.

At one point, I was following hundreds of body builders and fitness competitors to gain a better understanding of health and fitness. It was fantastic, the information and education I was drawing from it was worth more than money.

One thing that I could have done without, however, was all the 'Humpday' posts on Wednesdays. It seemed like a weekly occurrence where fitness competitors would post a picture of their ass on Wednesdays. Body builders would do it too. Yes, the world has changed.

Aside from the fitness industry, many industries joined in the fun and took to Social Media to expand their reach and platform. The financial industry for example, was a huge player in this game, still is. Financial planners and Gurus took to it and they wanted to make a big splash.

Other industries included real estate, catering, renovations, and the list goes on. Opening a page on Instagram to promote your business had become a thing. These days, we see it a lot. But 2014 is when we really started to see it and now it has become the norm. For anyone starting a business these days, you are urged to seek a presence on Social Media.

This year pretty much marked the shift towards business on Social Media as a whole. If you think about it, Facebook is generally used for personal purposes mostly. Instagram and Twitter are more commonly used for business. This isn't true all the time, but overall, that is what we see most of. There are still plenty of people that use Facebook as a tool to promote their business, but generally this is what you see.

With all these platforms we now have access to, each one is bound to be used for more specific purposes, especially for those who have businesses. Moving forward, Snap Chat is a medium all to its own, and vastly different than the 3 main ones we have discussed thus far. But let's save that for the next chapter ⍰.

CHAPTER 19
2015

Snap Chat was now making its mark! In 2012, Snap Chat users were sending 2 million to 3 million snaps per day. By 2015, that number had grown to over 6 billion snaps per day. That number has increased substantially today. That was a massive jump in numbers, but it shows how quickly things can escalate. My, that escalated quickly.

This was the year I entered the world of Snap Chat and I found it to be a lot of fun. Sending videos and pictures that could only be viewed in a 24-hour period. Before joining, I avoided it for a long time, but like I said before, the world is moving forward, you either get on the bus or you get left behind.

At this point, you would go out to all sorts of places, night clubs, malls, and anywhere public, you would see people taking real time snaps. In today's world, you see it all the time, but back in 2015, this was relatively new. Before this, you still would see people taking photos, either selfie or in groups, but videos were rarer. By 2015, the craze was on and everyone was making videos.

When I first started, a friend of mine gave me a tutorial on it and it didn't really interest me until I started using it myself. It gets exhausting viewing snaps all day, honestly it does. Getting used to it and knowing how to pace yourself is the key, not just with this platform, but with all Social Media platforms.

Some people got so into themselves that they would use other forms of Social Media to promote their Snap Chat. I remember one of my Facebook friends posting "Not gonna lie, my Snap story from last night was pretty epic." Like, who the fuck cares, that's what I was thinking.

It got to the point where everyone was out trying to out-do each other. Since it was still relatively new, this was a point in society when you would see some Snap stories that were public and quite provocative. These days, people do send provocative videos to each other, every day. But in 2015, people would routinely post videos of partial nudity, public affection, basically things I am not interested in seeing. Its better to just delete these people.

I have given examples in this book about other experiences and what I've seen on Social Media platforms, but I will not go into it here. The only thing I will say is that I saw too much nudity and sexual exploits of people that I had known for a long time, and it was almost enough to turn me off Snap Chat altogether.

On a more positive note, this platform did provide a wonderful way of sharing videos privately, when direct messaging, with the people you love. I found it a great tool to connect with friends and family who lived afar. It also gave you the opportunity to be creative in your messaging with them.

I would message with family that lived in different cities. We would always send each other videos of our homes, food, and fun times. I know it is like facetime calling, and it might seem that facetime calling would be better. But Snap Chat gives you the opportunity to be creative and send cool videos. And just in case you don't want these videos out in public, they would be unavailable after view or within 24 hours.

To this point, Snap Chat was by far the most fun form of Social Media. The ability to post videos at will was priceless. Everyone always wants to be a movie star, and now the entire world was getting the opportunity to start in their own Snap Stories.

2015 for Snap Chat was much like 2007 for Facebook, and 2012 for Instagram. Don't forget 2020 for Tik Tok, which we will get into more later in this book. There was a feeling out process for sure, and people were making bad decisions when posting. I am not going to sugar coat that; we've all been there.

In 2015, I can't tell you how many people asked me how high my 'Snap Score' was. LOL. I was never an avid user of Snap Chat, although I did and still do use it regularly. It seemed like everyone was in competition with this too, the Snap Score. And people were guarded about it too. I never was but witnessing the reactions of some people after they were asked about it was kind of funny.

It was almost as if you were asking them for their bank account password. They would get all standoffish and start questioning your motives. "Why are you asking?" Give me a break. By now, people had become very guarded with their

Social Media handles, so much so that they would get upset when you asked them certain questions, like the Snap Score.

I am happy that I joined Snap Chat and it has become such a fun platform to use. It is evolving as well, like all Social media is. Of all the platforms, I honestly wish I had created this one. It is quite simple, easy to use, and the privacy is worth it's weight in gold.

CHAPTER 20

2016

By 2016, the world was fucked. Seriously, things had changed so much. The reason I put a lot of emphasis on the years 2007 to 2016 in this book is because those were the formative years of worldwide Social Media. Anything that comes after this will not be received the same, because society is now conditioned to be aware and not post stupid shit (Mostly). Also, many things that were not considered socially acceptable in 2007 are now just that, socially acceptable.

In the years that followed 2016 and that will continue to follow, not much will change. The types of platforms may be different, but overall reaction from society will be more numb. Social Media has become part of our every day lives and that's a fact.

In 2016, Tik Tok was initially released. Basically, it's a platform where people perform in outrageous and highly entertaining videos. Public reaction to it was not the same as it was for the previous major platforms. There are 2 reasons to this, and the first one is the conditioning of society.

The second reason is because it is a platform that is known for outrageous posts! Many videos that we see on there would NEVER have been socially acceptable in 2007. With all that I have talked about earlier in this book, with people making stupid posts at the beginning of some of these platform releases, now there is a Social Media platform that encourages strange and crazy videos!

The world changed so much between 2007 to 2016 that we have finally got to the point of 'who gives a fuck.' I mean this with respect to what we see online. Nothing is off limits and it has pretty much been that way since 2016. I will make a bold prediction right now and say that it will be until at least 2025 when we see something come to the world of technology that will have an impact as strong as Social Media. I can confidently say that now, even knowing how much Social Media means to us.

2016 was the final year of the 'growth stage' of Social Media. Kids that were in kindergarten in 2007 were now teenagers entering the world of Social Media for the first time. They have been exposed to it since the beginning, seeing their parents and friends taking photos. They have a different view on it than someone who was already an adult in 2007.

Overall, you can call Social Media real, or you can call it fake, but no matter who you are, you are still the one logging in.

SECTION 3

THE
FUTURE

CHAPTER 21

CELEBRITY PARTICIPATION

As a sports fan and overall follower of world events, I must applaud a man like Lebron James. As a basketball player, he is one of the greatest of all time. no question about that. I might take some heat on this from his fans, but the greatest of all time, in my view, is Michael Jordan.

Nevertheless, a celebrity with the platform of Lebron James has the power to inspire and send a message to millions of people. What better way to do that than with Social Media? Almost from the beginning, Lebron James has used his celebrity status, through Social Media, to send out his message to the world. He has shown time and again that he is willing to go to bat for a worthy cause. Like many celebrities before him that have demanded change, he has done so in an admirable way.

Being able to post a statement, and in one moment have it viewed by millions of people worldwide, now that's powerful. He has not shied away from the spotlight and as well has not backed off his stance on certain issues. His form of celebrity participation is a shining example of how it can be used for the greater good.

Oftentimes, a celebrity will make a controversial statement on Social Media or possibly post an irresponsible picture. In the early days, we would see a lot of stories in the news of how a celebrity's account was 'hacked' and that was the reason for a picture or post that may have been deemed inappropriate.

Sometimes, even as the world moves forward with people learning lessons about what not to post, we still see celebrities making posts that will offend people in some way. It happens, and when people get emotional about certain topics, they tend to let their emotions get the better of them and they fly off the handle with what they put out there.

Personally, as a citizen of the free world, I do believe in the power of free speech. At the same time, I believe that if people want to post racial slander or any type of remarks that hurt certain groups of people (Such as LGBTQ or maybe even people of differing religious beliefs) then they should just delete their profiles and save the world from their needless immaturity. We don't need that shit.

We have seen both the good and the bad when it comes to celebrity participation in the world of Social Media. Moving forward, we will see better than bad. Why? Because saying stupid things in the public eye can ruin one's reputation or even end their career. Think about it, it's a no-brainer.

If I was a Major League Baseball player and it came out that one of my teammates was a racist, then I would not want that person on my team. I would ask management to trade him (or her) or I would seek a trade myself. There are no amounts of wins and losses that matter when you are sharing your life with someone of hate.

It has come to the point where celebrities are more careful with what they put out on Social Media, to the point where they are coached to keep from being stupid. Many of them have their assistants handle their posts as well. Social

Media has become so big that you now need an assistant to handle that, if you are rich and famous enough. Sometimes ⍰.

Back to positive, when celebrities decide to use their platform on Social Media to affect change in society, they are setting an example to the rest of the free world. That example is simple, it doesn't matter how rich or famous you are, we are all human and deserve to be treated fairly.

As of 2020, the undisputed king of Social Media was Cristiano Ronaldo. A celebrity, of course, and one of the greatest soccer players of his generation. His reach is well into the hundreds of millions. He can post anything he wants on Social Media and it will be seen by the entire world in a matter of seconds, amazing.

A guy like him has tons of endorsements and he regularly does 'paid partnership' posts. Also, he has regular posts that feature products he endorses, imagine the power he holds, with the platform he has. I talked earlier in this book about advertising on Social Media. Well this is the most powerful form of marketing on Social Media, using celebrities.

Before the age of Social Media, we would watch endless commercials on T.V. with celebrities endorsing products. Michael Jordan is perhaps the most famous mass athlete marketer of all time. In the 1990s, it seemed as though every 3rd commercial on T.V. was starring him. Commercials do exist and always will, but now they art posted on Social Media extensively.

Overall, celebrity participation on Social Media has become more of a business than just pleasure. While regular people like myself use Social Media to connect with friends, celebrities see it as form of business. Just like how other industries use Social Media for their businesses, celebrities can use it to make more money.

With this, hence the reason I applaud a man like Lebron James. He does understand the business of Social Media, but at the same time he will not undermine his own values just to make that extra dollar. His platform is not just about money, it's about making change.

CHAPTER 22

INFLUENCERS

Leading in from the last chapter, marketing in business has become almost the main purpose of Social Media in the modern world. With that, Social Media Influencers have come to the forefront to provide a viable option to those looking to expand their business, product, or service.

For those who don't have too much knowledge of this, an influencer is a person that either has a vast knowledge of a certain product which they are promoting, or they have a lot of social influence based on their name, family name.

Social Media influencers can be any form of celebrity, expert in their field, or even child of a celebrity that has a lot of followers because mommy or daddy are famous.

In today's world, we see Social Media influencers every day in many different forms. An extremely popular form of influencer is of the food industry. On smaller scales, we see people create pages on Instagram dedicated to restaurants they go to in the regions where they live. These are smaller, non-famous types of influencers, but they are a great example of what it means to influence on Social Media.

Every time I open my Instagram account, I see some sort of post relating to different foods being offered at restaurants which I follow. The posts are made by local influencers of course. I absolutely love these; I am a big fan of it. I am not necessarily a 'Foodie,' but seeing how creative people can get with food will always be an interest of mine.

Some of the more famous influencers in the world get involved in 'Paid Partnership' posts. People like Cristiano Ronaldo, Dwayne Johnson, or even the Kardashians. They would simply market a product by posting it on their page. Now, this is kind of a different level of influencing, it's more widely known as endorsing. But, nevertheless, it's a modern approach to marketing. Everyone is on Social Media, go where the masses can be found.

Going back to regular influencing, by that I mean non-famous people that have built up their Social Media accounts to the point where they are looked upon as people that can have an impact on consumer product selection. The influencers that have built up their Social Media to high levels tend to ask for fees when they post products.

'Pay per post.' Have you ever heard that term? In 2007, it wasn't a common term. In 2014, it wasn't a common term. By 2016 and beyond, it became part of the very fabric of online marketing. People that have high numbers of followers are now able to charge money for their posts. Of course, true influencers would never market products they don't believe in. At least, that is my viewpoint on that.

Business is business. The direct marketing approach is an immensely powerful way to get to the demographic of consumers that you are looking for. Influencers can really have a positive effect on your product or service, no doubt. This approach can become a very costly way to do business, but it's important to note that the reach in which Social Media can bring you can be unmatched when it comes to other forms of advertising.

I am not an expert on Social Influencers, but I can say with confidence that they bring an especially important and modern approach to the way business is done today. Looking to the future, it will continue to become more important with the evolution of Social Media and the way people go about interacting with it.

As an avid Social Media user, I have totally purchased products that I initially seen through an influencers post. In fact, sometimes I seek out the influencers and view their posts in order to help me gain a better understanding of the product I'm buying. Don't hesitate to ask them questions, they are there to help you!

CHAPTER 23

GOING LIVE

In 2016, Facebook introduced 'Going Live' to the world, and it was a hit! Out of seemingly nowhere, people were doing their own live videos for the world to see. As we all know, with these, you can not edit before it hits the world stage. Risk level – 100.

Every day I opened my account, there was someone going live. It was quite funny at first as people were still getting used to the idea. There were your expected hiccups and such. It almost seemed like people didn't think anyone would watch, and they would proceed to do or say something stupid. I know you can see who is watching and how many people are watching, but still, with a new medium comes new fuckups.

In the mere days that 'Going Live' was introduced, I was out late one night and got home after midnight. I opened my page and saw someone was on live, a person on my friends list that I barely knew. They were out with some friends and recording themselves on the app. Normally, it wouldn't be a big thing, but this was different. They were committing a crime with their friends!

They were all drunk and were spray painting street signs all over town! I got bored after a couple of minutes and went to sleep. By the next morning, these guys were arrested! It turns out, they were recording for over an hour, and someone called the authorities on them. Tough shit, but that's what you get for being cocky.

In the years following the introduction, there have been many instances where the 'Going Live' feature has shown situations of a highly graphic nature. There have been instances where people have been killed while being recorded on Facebook Live. This is inhumane and completely malicious. Showing things like this was not what this feature was intended for.

Seeing things like this on the news makes my stomach turn. It really can show a dark side of the world that many of us never want to see. In the modern day, we can pretty much see anything online, and I did watch one of these recordings after the fact, I will not say which one. I honestly wish I hadn't. I didn't sleep for a week; people can be very mean.

On a lighter note, I have gotten to watch many great and inspiring videos on live. At a wedding one time that I attended, the Bride and Groom streamed their wedding on Facebook so that family who were overseas had the ability to witness the event. That was at the beginning, it's now been done millions of times. I must admit though, seeing that for the first time was cool and it showed how the world was indeed getting smaller.

Into the future, I hope people are more careful with 'Going Live' and the people who use it to record stupid and disgusting things, well they should be banned. With the good always comes a few bad apples that want to spoil the party. There's nothing we can do about that, posting live will always be at our disposal, so we can only do our best to control what we watch and who we add.

CHAPTER 24

FACEBOOK

Facebook will always be the standard online website that every programmer in the world would aspire to create. Something that has had the same impact or beyond. As I have predicted earlier in this book, by 2025, something will come along that will make an impact just as big, or even bigger than Facebook.

There are no absolutes when it comes to the human mind. We can achieve accomplishments well beyond our wildest dreams. As true as this statement is, taking it further, there are no absolutes to the human heart. The person who cracks this code and discovers or develops something bigger, is going to be someone who was not born yet when Windows 95 was first introduced to the world.

In the online world, Mark Zuckerberg stands alone at the mountaintop, the unquestioned king of Social Media. He had the heart to go after it, and he made it happen. But someone will step up and take that crown from him, you better believe it. Right now, somewhere in the world, there is a person who has the capabilities within themselves, they just haven't 'arrived' yet so to speak.

The initial shockwaves that Facebook created were tremendous and unseen before it's time. As it continues to evolve, people will keep finding uses for it and they will keep posting their photos. They will keep posting their videos. They will put 'likes' wherever they want. They will enjoy it too.

The privacy settings on Facebook have become very sophisticated over the years, so much so that a high percentage of people tend to use the settings to some degree. This is generally done for their personal pages. For business pages, no amount of privacy settings are needed, for obvious reasons.

The information, videos, and pictures posted on Facebook will be available forever. It will no longer be normal for someone to 'go upstairs to the attic to find their baby pictures.' All of that will be found online, on Facebook. In fact, by 2025, when people born into the Social Media era start getting married, we will find that the wedding slideshows will be epic. They will be full of high-quality photos and videos. Weddings will never be the same.

I have been to a lot of weddings in my lifetime, and rarely did I ever watch a wedding slideshow that had countless high-quality videos and pictures. Hopefully, I can get myself invited to more weddings in the future. I'd rather not have to crash them ▯.

Facebook also has become part of culture in many ways. It has become a real slap in the face to someone if you 'unfriend' them. In fact, in 2009, it was named as the 'word of the year.' Good riddance to those who unfriend you, it's not that big of a loss.

Becoming 'Facebook Official' became part of society a long time ago. Especially at the beginning, people that were getting into relationships were posting it on Facebook religiously. As time went on, people decided to keep their love lives more private. Don't get me wrong, you still see a lot of people going 'official' on Facebook, but with the amount of privacy controls that have been put in place, the things people are willing to show has become more selective.

In 2007, when meeting someone for the first time, you added them to Facebook. By 2020, when meeting someone for the first time, you likely didn't. Facebook has become a more private way of doing Social Media and there are many that keep it for friends and family, that's it.

From 2007 to 2009, I added hundreds of people to Facebook. By 2010, I didn't know half of these people personally. At nightclubs, on vacations, or even house parties. "Hey! Do you have Facebook?" That entire term was quite common in those years.

I love having Facebook. Being able to connect with friends and family on such a level just continues to amaze me. Watching them go through their lives and supporting them with 'likes.' When you have a positive circle, you witness positive things. Seeing weddings and births is an honour. Watching gross things is depressing.

In the future, Facebook will always be the standard bearer for what's next. We will eventually get to a point where over 90% of the world uses Facebook. Trust me, it will happen. If you genuinely think about it, go back to the early

1900s. How many homes had a television set? How many homes had a radio? How many homes had a car? How many homes had heat? How many homes had running water?

Facebook has changed the world. Plain and simple. I am proud to call myself an avid user of it, even though I am not constantly posting. Just remember, ladies and gentlemen, 90%. By the year 2035, this will be a true statement, 90% of the world will be using Facebook.

CHAPTER 25

TWITTER

Facebook for grown ups. This sums up what I thought about it before I even knew what it was all about. When I was a kid, McDonalds came out with the 'Arch Deluxe.' As a reader, if you are old enough to remember this product, then you know what I'm talking about. For those of you who don't know what I'm referring to or are too young to remember, I will enlighten you.

In the 1990s, McDonalds came out with the 'Arch Deluxe' hamburger that was designed to attract older customers. They called it a more 'grown up' taste. In fact, one commercial even had Ronald McDonald himself playing a round of golf. To this day, I still remember that specific commercial and how strange it was to watch Ronald McDonald swing a golf club.

McDonalds clearly had the market cornered when it came to the under-18 crowd. The demographic they were trying to reach was the adults, the ones who had 'grown out' of' McDonalds. Similarly, Twitter, it seemed to me anyway, was designed for people who thought Facebook was for younger people.

Twitter did attract a lot of older users and it did become a platform that was commonly used by businesses. Before Instagram became such a powerhouse, Twitter was dominating the business landscape on Social Media. Twitter, like Facebook, was here to stay. Unfortunately, McDonalds discontinued the 'Arch Deluxe.'

Both cases were similar yet had different outcomes. Twitter kept growing while the 'Arch Deluxe' died. In both cases, they were trying to attack an older audience. Why the differing result? Well, it all has to do with how new Social Media was, and how mature McDonalds was.

People were still discovering Social Media at that time, so older demographic people did give it a shot, because it was all so new. McDonalds, however, had been around over 40 years at that time, people had already been accustomed to the taste they had grown up with.

I have no doubt in my mind that if the 'Arch Deluxe' had been introduced to McDonalds in the 1950s, it would still be on the menu today. It was my favourite item on the menu. Interestingly, I was in high school at the time and I worked at a McDonalds in the summer. I decided to get creative one day, so I made myself a quadruple 'Arch Deluxe.' It took me 20 minutes to finish, and it made me sluggish for the rest of my shift. But, man oh man, it was worth it!

Twitter has continued to provide a platform for business to do business on Social Media. It is quite simple and easy to use. It is great for news and staying up on current events, perfect for an older crowd that likes to read.

I personally know a guy that was one of the first 1000 people to create an account on Twitter (So he claimed). I remember him urging me to try it, but I kept resisting. Eventually I 'gave in.' I enjoyed how simple and straight forward it was, not too complicated to use.

Over the years, Twitter has evolved, much like the other platforms that we have. At the same time, it has kept its core in place and the changes it has made have not been very drastic. Twitter has its place in the world of Social Media.

The 'Twitter Bird' is by far the most famous of the Social Media branding logos. They got this right. It's a lot like other logos in modern business, Nike, the Jordan Brand, and the Golden Arches of McDonalds to name a few. With all these logos, you know exactly what brand you are looking at without hesitation.

When Twitter was first starting to make an impact, you'd see that little blue bird everywhere. It was painted on cars, I'd see graffiti with the design in subway terminals, and every now and then, you'd see people walking through carnivals with that little blue bird as face paint on people's cheeks!

People like Shaquille O'Neal were credited with really pushing Twitter at the beginning. The developers did a great job in putting together a great platform, but having celebrities push the use of these Social Media platforms in the beginning was huge. Regular people like me always look to what celebrities are doing, that's just the way it is.

I will be honest, I don't use Twitter as much as I use the other platforms, but I do use it and find it extremely helpful in business. I think anyone that is not using Twitter is missing out. The younger generation does tend to use the other platforms as they do offer more creativity. At the same time, there will not be any new platforms coming down the pipe that can maintain the popularity of Twitter while being 'simple.' Twitter has the market cornered on that.

CHAPTER 26

INSTAGRAM

All hail the mighty Instagram, or 'IG.' The fourth most downloaded mobile app of the 2010s. Originally launched in 2010, this platform has become a standard for use by younger generation people that want to network socially, yet at the same time still maintain some sort of privacy. It some respects, it can be considered a healthy alternative to Facebook, even though Facebook owns them.

You can do everything on this platform. Posting pictures, posting videos, posting long written posts, and going live. You also have your Instagram story, much like Snap Chat stories. (You can also do this on Facebook). It seems to combine a lot of what Facebook and Snap Chat do, but in a different way, I'll explain.

Comparing to Facebook, you can do pretty much everything Facebook offers, only your profile name can be whatever you want it to be. As we all know, Facebook shows your real name, or it should. In the beginning there were a lot of people who had 'one-letter last names.' You would see a 'Michael N.' or a 'Stephanie R.' It was common and it was annoying.

Comparing to Snap Chat, you still can post stories. But the difference is that you can post things on Instagram that can stay on your page if you so choose. I guess they must be different, because if they all fully copied each other, they'd end up in court.

The biggest feature that is attracting Instagram to the masses is that you can hold multiple accounts. This is great for business and people that want to build their brand. Also, you see a lot of Instagram users who have a personal page separate from their business page. This is fantastic and many young entrepreneurs have jumped at this.

This has led to some people to create 'burner accounts' in order to anonymously post hurtful things, harass people, or even build up their other accounts under false pretense. In 2017, Kevin Durant, a multiple-time NBA All Star, was accused of having burner accounts and using them to defend his name and real account. He took a lot of heat for it. Honestly, who gives a fuck, let the man live his life.

It has come to the point in society that when certain celebrities 'unfollow' each other on Instagram, it creates worldwide headlines in the news. It's almost like life or death. "Oh my God! Cristiano Ronaldo has unfriended Ariana Grande! What are we going to do!?" Because they are celebrities, we care.

Instagram will continue to grow. If people can always be creative with their profile names, they will continue to use it and post more risky material. They will leave Facebook to family.

CHAPTER 27

SNAP CHAT

I personally created my Snap Chat account in 2015. I'll be honest, one of the main types of 'Snap Stories' I hated was when people posted endless videos of the raves they were at. I am not a person who attends these types of events, so maybe I'm missing something here. But watching endless videos of lights blaring didn't feel like an ideal use of my time.

In the year 2015, you would see endless amounts of people making videos on Snap Chat everywhere. As I have mentioned earlier in this book, at the beginning, everyone was out to create the greatest Snap story ever, it was on.

One situation that I encountered left me speechless. I pulled up to a red light and there was a homeless man begging for spare change. Every time cars would stop at the red light; he would go to the windows and ask for money. By the time he got to my car, I decided to help the man out and I reached for my spare change.

Growing up, I was a big fan of Professional Wrestling. So, on that day, I was wearing an 'AUSTIN 3:16' shirt. It turned out this guy was a wrestling fan as well. The second he laid eyes on my shirt; his eyes lit up. Then, he began to talk. Word for word, this is what he said.

"Hey man I love Steve Austin! Do you wrestle? I used wrestle to in high school but then I hurt my knee. I was going pro if I didn't get hurt."

It was at this point he pulled an iPhone out of his pocket. I figured it was stolen and thought he was going to try and sell it to me. Then he uttered the words I never thought I'd hear a homeless man say.

"Can you be in my Snap Story?"

This guy was homeless, begging for money in the street, yet he had his own cell phone? At this point I thought he was a con man, but I went along with it anyways. The light was red for a long time. He put up is iPhone and had the both of us within the camera centre. He started recording and then just as he was about to talk, I put up both my middle fingers, looked directly at the camera, and said, "Fuck you." I then drove off.

By 2020, you started to see funny and 'kidlike' Snap Chat profile names. That is because you had people turning 18 who started their Snap Chat when they were like 12. I liken this back to the late 1990s when email started to become a big thing. After a few years, people who opened their accounts as teens or pre-teens, they would have interesting Hotmail or Gmail names.

At the turn of the century, I was still in school and teachers would adamantly push the fact that you needed a new email account if your existing one sounded strange. This was to prepare you for the world of work and putting your email address on your resume had now become common. Having a 'kidlike' email account didn't come across as professional.

In the real world, you don't normally see people putting their Social Media handles on their resumes. But businesses, however, do put their Social Media handles on their websites and post it throughout their Social Media pages. This is the new world.

Snap Chat itself has become extremely popular, with the United States being the country holding the most users. Making videos and movies at the touch of your finger. It's nowhere near what Facebook and Instagram are when it comes to Alexa Rank, but it is here to stay.

As I have alluded to earlier in this book, Snap Chat has become a popular way of users sharing private content of a sexual nature directly. It used to be people sending nudes to each other, men and women alike. But there were too many controversies among celebrities in the pre-Snap Chat era.

There can only be so many 'leaked' nude photos of celebrities until we finally, as a society, get the hint. At one point, it seemed like a different celebrity every week was on the news because of some sort of nude photo they sent to an ex boyfriend or ex girlfriend. I'm sure that is rather embarrassing.

With text, you can screenshot photos and save them too, along with saving videos. Everyone in the free world knows that. Eventually, people started to get smarter and send pictures that didn't show their faces. Still, though, you will be recognized by someone out there.

Snap Chat provided a new medium for people to privately send photos and videos of whatever they like. And if a person screenshotted what you sent; you would know about it. There are millions of sexual videos and pictures being sent every day on Snap Chat.

To each their own, that's what I always say. By the way, to get around the entire 'screenshot' notification, some people carry 2 phones so that they can take a video or picture of what was sent, without the sender knowing. This is fucked, but it is reality. To everyone out there sending this type of material, just be careful!

CHAPTER 28

TIK TOK

Here we go. Tik Tok is a video sharing platform and a form of Social Media that bases itself on creativity. It gives the user the ability to create their own music videos and videos of all sorts. There are many features that it comes with that help put your idea into reality. Overall, it's just a fun platform.

Initially released in 2016, it has exploded on the scene, much like its predecessors. In 2007, we would have never thought that a platform like this would be possible, people sharing wild and crazy videos. Now, this isn't the 'Girls Gone Wild' type of stuff, but it is fun to watch some of these outlandish videos come to life.

The number of features that are available on this platform that help add life to your videos is just awesome. People all over the world are having fun with this, and isn't that what it's all about? I remember from 2014-2017, millions of people were using Social Media to create havoc and make their exes jealous. That was not what it was ever intended for, but that's life.

Tik Tok has not gotten to the point where people will use it to make videos to hurt others, but who knows? Anything is possible with Social Media. Comparing it, I guess people can use these videos to do some damage to others, but what's the point? People are having too much fun with it, let them.

The NFL signed a deal with Tik Tok in 2019 to help attract a younger fanbase. So, they have all sorts of promotions that they will be doing. For an institution like the National Football League, a league that has been around over 100 years, to partner with a Social Media platform that is in its baby years, that tells you something. The world has changed.

Since I joined Tik Tok myself, I have noticed something. There are a lot of talented people in this world that are great dancers! I'll tell you guys one thing, that ain't me. I know this is not proper English, but seriously, I will never subject the world to my dance moves. Just won't happen. ⍰.

I do appreciate the videos I see, and I will likely post videos that show my other skills, such as public speaking, but I'll leave it at that. I'll save my indulgence for the next great Social Media phenomenon. Tik Tok, like all the other Social Media platforms, is a lot of fun. In fact, it may be the most entertaining platform yet. We'll see what the future brings.

CHAPTER 29
THE CLASS OF 2025

For all those born in 2007, you were born into a world that had already succumbed to the presence of Social Media. That was a year where the world changed, and I have made sure to put some serious emphasis on it. In 2025, the graduating high school class of North America will be mostly made up of people born in that very year, 2007.

In January, the iPhone was first announced by Steve Jobs. It was released in June. In today's world, the iPhone is one of the most popular products ever created. The ease in which its use helps us get online and enjoy all the wonderful 'Apps' at our disposal. This was the start of something big, as this initial announcement will continue to have waves well into the future.

In February, Tumblr, a blogging Social Media site was established. Although I don't get into it much in this book, Tumblr has had an impact and maintains an extremely high Alexa rank. It clearly never took off the way Instagram did, but nevertheless, it has made an impact on the online world. Blogging is big business.

The world financial crisis started in 2007, and countries around the world felt the pinch, Greece being one of the most publicised cases at the time. The world really didn't feel it until 2008, but the steps in 2007 led to the eventual demise. It got so bad; many people wondered if the economy would ever rebound. It eventually did, but not until years later.

At that time, the greatest basketball player in the world was Kobe Bryant. The greatest hockey player in the world was Sidney Crosby. The greatest soccer player in the world was Zinedine Zidane. The fastest man in the world was Tyson Gay of the United States. The U.S. President was George W. Bush. Barack Obama was starting to come into his own as an internationally recognized figure and was poised to run for President the next year.

By the time this class graduates in 2025, there will be a lot of things that did not exist in their lifetimes as a needed commodity. The ever-changing world has provided us countless items of value that has made products of past years obsolete.

I bet if you put a rotary phone in front of one of these kids, they either won't know what it is or they simply would wonder how we lived by communicating in that basic manner, without a cell phone. Put a typewriter in front of them and they might mistake it for a musical instrument. You'd be surprised.

Other than the iPhone, the following list of items did not exist in 2007.

- Tinder
- Doordash
- Pinterest
- 4G
- Airbnb
- Netflix Originals
- Uber
- Instagram
- Snap Chat
- Tik Tok
- iPads
- Ironman had yet to be released
- Bitcoin
- The Selfie Stick

- Spotify
- The term 'Stay Woke'
- Tesla

As you can see, the world has changed rapidly, and it is going to continue in that trend. The class of 2025 will be subject to all different types of technology the previous generation didn't have access to. Imagine living in a world that does not have access to all the items I have listed. For you and me, we lived through the constant changes that came. For the class of 2025, they won't know any other world.

I already mentioned that the next person that will change the online world was not even born by the time Windows 95 came out. It is a very real possibility that the next Mark Zuckerberg will be a person that was born in 2007.

In 1955, 3 of the most important contributors to the online world, were born. Bill Gates, Steve Jobs, and Tim Berners-Lee came into this world and they changed it by the time they reached adulthood. Tim Berners-Lee was the inventor of the World Wide Web just in case you were wondering. The other 2 guys, you know who they are.

The class of 2025 will learn about the fast track the world took to get online systems and turn them into reality. They will learn about the conditions we all lived in, and it was normal. Cell phones did not really exist on a mainstream level until the late 1990s, well before the Social Media era.

I know many of you may be thinking it's the class of 2022 that I should be talking about because Facebook was started in 2004. But let's be real here, 2007 was key year when everything exploded. Being able to document our daily lives, every minute of every day, essentially started with the introduction of the iPhone. Now, every day I can open one of my apps and see multiple friends documenting their days via Snap Chat or Instagram stories. From paper cuts to graduations, I see it all.

I honestly don't know the world statistics on this, but in the United States, more babies were born in 2007 than in any other year in history up until that point, and the previous high was in 1957, right at the height of the baby boomer era. There are all sorts of theories as to why. Personally, I think it had something to do with the world economy being at a boom (Keep in mind the financial crisis did start in 2007, but people were getting pregnant in 2006 and early 2007 to make the high number of births possible).

People were making money, having fun, and having lots of sex. There's just something about having tons of cash that makes people horny. LOL just kidding. If you honestly think about it, that statement could be true. At the same time, when people are in a good financial position, they are not as scared to become parents. They feel more comfortable bringing a child into this world knowing they can support them.

The class of 2025 will be a big one. They were born into a world that was changing more rapidly than ever. Never had the modern world had a year like this. The rise of an international phenomenon, Social Media, coupled with the crash of the world economy. These babies were just bound for different.

A friend of mine recently told me something interesting. His kids are teenagers and their family is awfully close. I have known him for many years and watched his kids grow up. They are teenagers as of 2020. His oldest son has him blocked on Facebook. I was a little taken aback when he told me this, although he seemed to find it amusing. I did as well.

A few weeks later I was over at their home, and his oldest son was home. I asked him about him having his father blocked. We were all in the room chatting. He said that his dad started commenting on his pictures with his girlfriend and it was 'embarrassing.' Boy, we all had a laugh after him saying that. Remember, things are different between parents and their children when the child is 15 years old and an adolescent, compared to when the child in 25 years old and an adult. I'm sure by the time he is finished college he will unblock his father and the world can be normal again.

CHAPTER 30
THE LONG TERM EFFECTS

One major concern I have always had was the fact that communication will become a lost art in the world we know today. Think about it, everyone growing up has been able to hide behind a text message or Social Media. Everyone has an opinion. When I was growing up, if you said something insulting to someone, expect to be met outside in the parking lot to defend what you say. These days, people stay home and talk shit on Social Media.

I worry about future generations that will have issues trying to communicate 'person to person.' Going on a date with a person born in 1981 is a hell of a lot different than going on a date with a person born in 1997. The person born in 1981 will want to talk and chat it up. The person born in 1997 will want to check their phone every 10 minutes for status updates and messages. This isn't true all the time, I'm just giving a basic example.

Before 2007, breaking up with someone over text was really starting to become a hot hobby. People all over the world were taking advantage of this medium and it really pissed people off. Heck, even I got dumped over text once in 2004. At first, I was confused and thought it was a joke. Then, once I realized it was not a joke, I was upset and hurt. How could people be so mean? Believe it, they can be that mean.

I was at the gym that day when the text came in. She got right to the point.

Girlfriend – We should start seeing other people.

Me – What?

Girlfriend – I wanted to tell you in person, but I couldn't.

Me – Let's meet up and talk about it.

Girlfriend – There's nothing to talk about. Let's just leave it at that.

Me – Leave it at what?

Girlfriend – Don't make this difficult please.

Me – But we just had sex last night! Everything seemed fine.

Girlfriend – I just have a lot of things going on in my life I need to focus on.

Me – Please tell me you're joking.

Girlfriend – I'm not. Goodbye.

Me – Hold on! This doesn't make any sense. You are breaking up over text?

Girlfriend – Please lets just be civil about this.

Me – Fuck civil. This just makes no sense.

Girlfriend – I'm sorry.

Me – Whatever.

We did end up talking on the phone after this because I called her. Clearly, I was upset, and a bit immature in my youth, but still it hurt. It really hurt. Keep in mind this was 2004, the pre-2007 world. Before Social Media. It took me a while to get over this but at the same time I learned that with the changing world, things like breakups could potentially start happening from afar.

In 2015, a friend of mine broke up with his girlfriend over a post she put up on Instagram. Funny thing, he said she rarely texted back right away anytime on regular text, but on the DM's, she would respond instantly. And boy oh boy, she responded damn quick on this. Perhaps it was the nature of the message, the breakup, but this just highlights the way the world is right now and beyond. People track their Social Media more than their regular phone contacts. He was pretty butt-hurt over the entire situation. I told him to 'cowboy up' and move on with his life. Both him and his girlfriend were in their 20s.

For people in the class of 2025, this will be a normal occurrence. Straight up, using Social Media to dump someone is and will be normal. There is now an arm's length between people here on earth, even though the world is getting smaller. The way people communicate has changed, but still, the person-to-person interaction has dwindled.

Sometimes, I get to thinking that the world of relationships will eventually come down to people only communicating remotely. Then, when it's time to get intimate, they meet up. I know this sounds crazy, but maybe 'pillow talk' will become a thing of the past as well? This might just be crazy talk, I know, but you just can't rule anything out. LOL.

I remember the movie 'DEMOLITION MAN' that starred Sylvester Stallone. It was set in 2032 (It was initially released in 1993) and it's a look to the future. In one scene, the character played by Sandra Bullock brings out a 'virtual sex simulator' when they are about to have sex. I honestly don't think it will ever come to that in an ultimate way, but who knows? You can count me out of that shit.

The long-term effects of Social Media really won't be felt until the first generational run-through. The class of 2025 will surely be an interesting one. They were born into this brave new world and they are part of a future that contains limitless possibilities. Hopefully, they stand up and don't hide behind their Social Media fortresses. Here's to them.

CONCLUSION

The Unreal World of Social media is whatever you want it to be, real, unreal, or fake. In the end, nobody is holding a gun to your head and forcing you to create a profile. You hold all the power at the tip of your finger. You can share your entire life story if you like, or you can boycott the entire industry. The choice is yours.

The evolution of Social Media in our world will just not stop. No matter how many people find joy in the status quo, and no matter how many people get hurt by seeing posts of their exes with someone else. As a society, moving forward will be the status quo, that's just the way it is.

To this point in my life, I have yet to post a picture with a famous world celebrity. If I could have chosen anyone in my lifetime, it would have surely been Mohammad Ali. For obvious reasons, he was a force that pushed for change in the past. Can you imagine there being Social Media when he was in his prime? Fighting for his rights and dodging the war based on his beliefs? "Why would I fight for you when you won't even fight for me here!" He wasn't dodging anything, he was standing up for his rights as a human being, against the institution that discriminated against him. Mohammad Ali and Social Media combined with the height of his fame as the World Heavyweight Champion... Imagine that.

Everyone wants to post pictures of themselves with celebrities. I have a friend that has a picture he took with Tupac Shakur. Yes, that's right, 2Pac himself. A picture taken in August of 1996 in southern California. He has it posted, and it's a 'one-of-a-kind' picture among regular people like us. I wish I were there with him that night.

With all the Social Media platforms available to us in modern day, one fact holds true. They are extremely addicting. In a way, I guess it can be like crack (I previously alluded to the 'crack book' nickname that Facebook had from 2007 to 2009), with a healthier twist. I have known many people that want to post non-stop, 365 days per year, 24 hours per day, and 7 days per week.

In society now, we do get people who decide to take a 'break' from Social Media and not post for 3 days or 6 days, or something of that nature. It has become such a part of society now that people want to take time away sometimes just to recharge their batteries. I can understand this, but it is up to each one of us to control our urges and keep it real.

Social Media is an addiction, but if used properly, can be a healthy one. Making memories is what life is all about. Remembering the great times is priceless. Facebook, Instagram, Snap Chat, Tik Tok, and all the rest of the platforms available to us make it possible to hold on to these moments forever. Enjoy your time on Social Media, no matter you see on there, keep it real. Life is just too short.

GENERAL MODERN TERMS

FYI	-	FOR YOUR INFORMATION
TY	-	THANK YOU
HMU	-	HIT ME UP
FU	-	FUCK YOU
TTYL	-	TALK TO YOU LATER
LMFAO	-	LAUGH MY FUCKEN ASS OFF
LMAO	-	LAUGH MY ASS OFF
LOL	-	LAUGH OUT LOUD
HAHA	-	HAHA
NM	-	NEVER MIND
C	-	SEE
U	-	YOU
B4	-	BEFORE
FML	-	FUCK MY LIFE
AKA	-	ALSO KNOWN AS
BTW	-	BY THE WAY
DIY	-	DO IT YOURSELF
FAQ	-	FREQUENTLY ASKED QUESTIONS
FTW	-	FOR THE WIN
IDK	-	I DON'T KNOW

NOYB	-	NONE OF YOUR BUSINESS
OMG	-	OH MY GOD
POV	-	POINT OF VIEW
TBA	-	TO BE ANNOUNCED
THX	-	THANKS
TYT	-	TAKE YOUR TIME
TTYL	-	TALK TO YOU LATER
WFM	-	WORKS FOR ME
WTF	-	WHAT THE FUCK
YMMD	-	YOU MADE MY DAY
AH	-	AT HOME
WBU	-	WHAT ABOUT YOU
APP	-	APPLICATION
AUW	-	AS YOU WISH
BC	-	BECAUSE
BRB	-	BE RIGHT BACK
DIY	-	DO IT YOURSELF
DL	-	DOWN LOW
DM	-	DIRECT MESSAGE
ETA	-	ESTIMATED TIME ARRIVAL
DTA	-	DON'T TRUST ANYONE
EZ	-	EASY

FB	-	FACEBOOK
IG	-	INSTAGRAM
FW	-	FORWARD
G2G	-	GOT TO GO
GF	-	GIRLFRIEND
BF	-	BOYFRIEND
GN	-	GOOD NIGHT
GR8	-	GREAT
STR8	-	STRAIGHT
HBU	-	HOW ABOUT YOU
HW	-	HOME WORK
GTG	-	GOT TO GO
ILY	-	I LOVE YOU
IMHO	-	IN MY HUMBLE OPINION
JC	-	JUST CHECKING
JK	-	JUST KIDDING
KK	-	OKAY
GB	-	GOD BLESS
DGMR	-	DON'T GET ME WRONG
MSG	-	MESSAGE
OMW	-	ON MY WAY
PM	-	PRIVATE MESSAGE

RU	-	ARE YOU
SRY	-	SORRY
TMRW	-	TOMORROW
TBL	-	TEXT BACK LATER
TC	-	TAKE CARE
W/O	-	WITHOUT
WTG	-	WAY TO GO

THE

UNREAL

WORLD

OF

SOCIAL

MEDIA